LUKE 2:1-18 FOR CHILDR

Written by Frances C. Allan

Illustrated by Jim Roberts

The Little Mouse's Wonderful Journey

Concordia Publishing House

ARCH Books

© 1972. All rights reserved.

CONCORDIA PUBLISHING HOUSE LTD.,

117/123 GOLDEN LANE, LONDON EC1Y OTL

Printed in England.

ISBN 0-570-06069-9

Clip-Clop was a donkey,
and Timmy was a mouse.
The little barn they lived in
was back of Mary's house.

Mary was a gentle girl
and not afraid of mice;
she left him honeycake to eat
and other things as nice.

One morning Timmy lay asleep
on some of Clip-Clop's straw —
eyes tightly shut, mouth open wide,
his head upon one paw.

While dreaming he heard Clip-Clop bray,
"Hee-haw! Hee-haw! Hee-haw!"
Then Timmy opened up his eyes,
surprised at what he saw.

Clip-Clop had his saddle on,
ready for a trip;
his bellyband was pulled quite tight,
so that it wouldn't slip.

"Where are you going?" Timmy asked.
"I don't know," Clip-Clop replied.
"But see that basket on the ground?
Why don't you get inside?

"No matter where I'm going,
I would like to have you along.
Besides, you weigh almost nothing at all,
while I am big and strong."

So Timmy did as Clip-Clop said,
and the basket soon was tied,
along with clothes and other things,
tightly to Clip-Clop's side.

Then Joseph, Mary's husband, said,
"Let's not forget the food.
That's all!" he cried. "We're ready!
Everything looks good!"

They travelled several days and nights
past hills and woods and streams
to a city much more wonderful
than Timmy's wildest dreams.

The city was full of people!
There were people everywhere!
There were crowds and crowds of people —
all Timmy could do was stare.

"What is the name of this city?
Where have you brought little me?"
"I'm not too sure of it," said Clip-Clop,
"But I know it begins with 'B.'"

Now, the city was so filled with people
that no place to sleep could be found,
and poor Mary and Joseph walked everywhere,
around and around and around.

At last they found an innkeeper,
with a long, white beard on his chin,
who said, "I'm sorry to tell you,
there is no room in my inn.

"But if you are not too fussy,
I do believe I am able
(for a very small sum of money)
to let you sleep in the stable."

Now Mary and Joseph were tired,
and Timmy was tired too.
They went to the stable and opened the door,
and the first thing they heard was a "MOO!"

There were cows in the stable, and donkeys and goats
and noisy geese and white sheep.
But in spite of the noise they laid themselves down,
and in minutes they all were asleep.

All but Timmy.

Timmy did not like the noise.
"I'll go outside," he said,
"and find a nice, soft clump of grass
and use that for a bed."

He crept outside and down the street
and trotted out of town.
He ran through fields and up a hill
and finally lay down.

Timmy soon fell fast asleep,
his head upon one paw.
Then suddenly he woke again,
surprised at what he saw.

Shepherds all around him stood;
the sky was filled with light,
and a voice said, "Christ the Saviour
has been born this very night!"

The shepherds then all hurried off
as fast as they were able
and Timmy followed, surprised to find
they led him to the stable.

The shepherds knelt before a Child
and said: "This wondrous light
is the same light we saw shining
in the fields tonight.

"This blessed Child is surely Christ,
the Son of God," they said.
"How strange the King, our Lord, has but
a manger for a bed!"

Then Mary glanced at Timmy,
who had come in from the street,
and saw the little mouse from home
between dear Clip-Clop's feet.

She smiled at him, and Timmy said:
"Oh, Clip-Clop, I'm so glad
you brought me on this lovely trip,
the best I ever had!"

DEAR PARENTS:

Christmas is for the animal world too. It is a happy part of the world of children — and fantasy can convey many a meaningful thought to the child.

Think of a story like this one as a kind of parable. Let the little mouse help your child to identify with the small and beloved creatures as they bask in the dazzling wonder of the Saviour's birth. For the love that Jesus brings to the world is meant to spread from the blessed children of God also to His animal world.

There is another lesson in this story. As the animals render joyful praise and willing service to their Lord by instinct, God's children can do so by choice. And this is the kind of love that means so much to Him.

Let that Christmas Eve, when even the animals and stones could hardly keep from singing, inspire your child to make up his own story in which he is the main character who arrives in his own way at the manger in wonder and joy.

THE EDITOR